SPORTS IN ACTION

YOGA

in Action

Kelley MacAulay & Bobbie Kalman

Photographs by Marc Crabtree

Crabtree Publishing Company

www.crabtreebooks.com

Created by Bobbie Kalman

Dedicated by Bobbie Kalman
For Andrea and Samantha, my yoga-loving daughters
Be flexible, be positive, be healthy, be joyful, be loving. Be true to you!

Editor-in-Chief
Bobbie Kalman

Writing team
Kelley MacAulay
Bobbie Kalman

Substantive editor
Kathryn Smithyman

Editors
Molly Aloian
Robin Johnson
Reagan Miller

Design
Vanessa Parson-Robbs

Cover design
Vanessa Parson-Robbs
Samantha Crabtree

Production coordinator
Heather Fitzpatrick

Photo research
Crystal Foxton

Consultants
Tony Sanchez, Yoga Master
    Director, US Yoga Association
Sandy Wong-Sanchez
    Program Director, US Yoga Association

Special thanks to
Lucia Leone, Peter Leone, Susan Leone, Keith Makubuya, Emily Murphy,
Zach Murphy, Jerry Leone, Candice Murphy, Michelle Hallé-Socha, Kyra Watters,
Rich Merlino, and White Oaks Conference Resort & Spa

Illustrations
Barbara Bedell: page 24
Bonna Rouse: page 23
Margaret Amy Salter: pages 13, 18, 19

Photographs
All photographs by Marc Crabtree except:
Corel: page 12 (mountain); Comstock: page 7 (all except girl); Creatas: page 20 (lion);
Digital Vision: pages 17 (frog), 22 (snake); Eyewire: page 16 (eagle); Photodisc: page 26 (cow)

Crabtree Publishing Company
www.crabtreebooks.com   1-800-387-7650

Copyright © **2006 CRABTREE PUBLISHING COMPANY.**
All rights reserved. No part of this publication may be
reproduced, stored in a retrieval system or be transmitted in
any form or by any means, electronic, mechanical, photocopying,
recording, or otherwise, without the prior written permission
of Crabtree Publishing Company. In Canada: We acknowledge
the financial support of the Government of Canada through
the Book Publishing Industry Development Program (BPIDP)
for our publishing activities.

Cataloging-in-Publication Data
MacAulay, Kelley.
    Yoga in action / Kelley MacAulay & Bobbie Kalman; photographs by Marc Crabtree.
        p. cm. -- (Sports in action series)
    Includes index.
    ISBN-13: 978-0-7787-0344-0 (rlb)
    ISBN-10: 0-7787-0344-4 (rlb)
    ISBN-13: 978-0-7787-0364-8 (pbk)
    ISBN-10: 0-7787-0364-9 (pbk)
    1. Hatha yoga. I. Kalman, Bobbie. II. Title. III. Sports in action
    RA781.7M3955 2005
    613.7'046--dc22
                                            2005020746
                                            LC

**Published in
the United States**
PMB16A
350 Fifth Ave.
Suite 3308
New York, NY
10118

**Published
in Canada**
616 Welland Ave.,
St. Catharines, Ontario
Canada
L2M 5V6

**Published in the
United Kingdom**
73 Lime Walk
Headington
Oxford
OX3 7AD
United Kingdom

**Published
in Australia**
386 Mt. Alexander Rd.,
Ascot Vale (Melbourne)
VIC 3032

Contents

What is yoga?

The word "yoga" means "union." Yoga helps **unite**, or bring together, your body and your mind. There are five main styles of yoga, and each style is different. **Karma Yoga** is a style of yoga that emphasizes being kind and helpful to others, while expecting nothing in return. **Raja Yoga** is a style of yoga that focuses mainly on **meditation**. Another style of yoga, **Jnana Yoga**, focuses on gaining wisdom. **Bhakti Yoga** is the yoga of **devotion** to a religion. The style of yoga shown in this book is called **Hatha Yoga**. Hatha Yoga is an ancient form of exercise.

Hatha Yoga

Hatha Yoga is a system of *asanas*, or physical poses, and breathing techniques. Together, these poses and techniques promote health and relaxation. Our minds move quickly, jumping from thought to thought. Holding Hatha Yoga poses helps you focus your mind on the present moment. Practicing yoga poses helps you both strengthen your body and calm your mind!

Boys who practice yoga are called **yogis**.
Girls who practice yoga are called **yoginis**.

Why practice yoga?

People practice yoga for many reasons. Yoga stretches your muscles. Stretching helps your body stay fit and **flexible**. Having a flexible body allows you to move easily, improves your **posture**, and keeps your **joints** and muscles healthy. Having a fit, flexible body can also improve your performance in many kinds of sports. Regular yoga practice may even help you in your studies at school! It can help you concentrate better and feel calmer each day.

Ancient history

People have been practicing yoga for over 5,000 years! Yoga was developed in northern India by **sages**, or wise people. For thousands of years, the practices and beliefs of the sages were not written down. Instead, they were passed down from teachers to students. About 2,000 years ago, a sage named Patanjali organized and wrote down the yoga practices and beliefs in a collection of writings called the *Yoga Sutras*. These writings allowed many people to learn about yoga. Today, yoga is one of the most popular forms of exercise!

A yoga lifestyle

Proper exercise

The principle of proper exercise is based on the idea that our bodies are meant to move around! Practicing yoga asanas strengthens your muscles, bones, and joints. Proper exercise is a fun and healthy part of life!

Some people practice yoga simply to stay fit and keep their muscles flexible. For other people, however, yoga is a **lifestyle**. A lifestyle is a way of living that reflects what you believe and what you feel is important. When you live a yoga lifestyle, your yoga practice continues throughout the day, even when you are not practicing asanas.

Proper principles

Living a yoga lifestyle can help keep you feeling happy, healthy, and connected to other people. To live a yoga lifestyle, you must follow the five **principles** of yoga—proper exercise, proper relaxation, proper diet, proper breathing, and positive thinking. Read these pages to find out more about the five principles of yoga. Following these principles will help you develop confidence, discipline, concentration, and patience.

Proper relaxation

Following the principle of proper relaxation means taking some time each day to relax and to let go of the worries in your life. By letting go of your worries, you will feel happier and have more energy.

Proper diet

Proper diet means eating nutritious foods such as fruits, vegetables, and whole grains. These foods give your body energy. Proper diet also means eating only when you are hungry. People often snack on sugary foods when they are nervous or bored. Sugary foods give you a short burst of energy, but you soon feel tired after the snack. Eating only when you are hungry and eating nutritious foods will keep you feeling energetic all day long.

Proper breathing

Without even noticing, you take many breaths each day! Proper breathing means **inhaling**, or breathing in, deeply and slowly and then pushing out the air completely when you **exhale**, or breathe out. Deep, slow breathing makes you feel relaxed and helps you concentrate.

Positive thinking

The principle of positive thinking means deciding to see the good in people and in situations. Practicing Hatha Yoga every day keeps you physically fit and helps you stay calm and positive. By staying positive, you will feel happier and more relaxed. Staying positive will also help you stay healthy!

Yoga basics

You can practice yoga at home or in a yoga studio. If you practice yoga at home, you will need a book or a video that teaches you how to perform yoga poses safely. If you prefer to practice yoga in a group, you can take yoga classes. Most yoga studios offer beginner classes for young yoga students. Make sure the instructor at the studio is properly **certified** to teach Hatha Yoga and that he or she has been practicing yoga for many years. If you choose to practice yoga in a yoga studio, you must follow the studio's rules.

These rules help prevent injuries and ensure that all students behave properly in the studio. The rules may include arriving for class on time, tying back long hair before beginning yoga practice, and respecting your instructor and classmates by remaining quiet while in the studio.

Different people practice yoga at different times of the day. Some people practice in the morning to help them feel alert and ready for the day. Other people practice in the evening to help them relax and get a good night's sleep. It is best to practice yoga every day, even if you have time to perform only a few poses.

Packing light

You do not need much equipment to practice yoga. Wear comfortable clothing such as stretchy pants or shorts. These clothes will not get in your way as you move. You also need a **yoga mat**, which is a long, sticky rubber mat. The yoga mat keeps your feet from slipping as you practice. If you do not have a yoga mat, you can spread out a towel on which to perform your yoga poses. If you borrow a sticky mat from your studio, you may want to spread a towel over the mat before you begin practicing.

Yoga is practiced barefoot. Practicing barefoot allows you to grip the floor with your feet, so you will not slip.

Your own pace

Yoga is not about competition! Do not worry if the person beside you is more flexible or seems to perform the poses better than you can. With regular practice, your body will become more flexible, and the poses will become easier to do. It is important to listen to your body and practice at your own skill level. Never push yourself too hard and make sure you do not feel pain when you stretch. Also, remember to have fun!

Mind and body as one

Practicing yoga poses is only one part of bringing the mind and body together. Breathing exercises and meditation should also be regular parts of your practice. Breathing exercises and meditation help calm your mind, making it easier and more enjoyable for you to perform the yoga poses.

It's all in the breath

When you practice yoga, breathing properly is as important as performing the poses properly. The way you breathe can greatly affect the way you feel. Taking deep breaths adds **oxygen** to your blood, making you feel relaxed and clear-headed. Yoga breathing exercises teach you to pay attention to your breathing, which reminds you to take enough deep breaths each day. Breathing exercises are always done through the nose. Breathing through your nose slows down your breathing, which helps you get full, deep breaths. Also, the hairs in your nose filter dirt from the air and warm up the air before it reaches your lungs.

Better breathing

To make sure you never hold your breath while you perform yoga poses, focus on your breathing. A great way to begin your practice is with a breathing exercise. To begin, lie on your back with your knees bent and your feet flat on the floor. Place your hand on your chest so you can feel your breathing. As you inhale, expand your **abdomen** and then your chest. Next, pull in your abdomen as you exhale all the air from your lungs. Repeat this breathing exercise ten times.

Calming the active mind

To experience the full benefits of yoga, you must be able to calm your mind. One of the best ways to calm your mind is through meditation. Meditation is an exercise in which you focus your mind and allow your thoughts to slow down. Focus on your breathing as you meditate. Focusing on your breathing will make you aware of your body and how it feels. You will notice how good you feel as you take deep breaths of clean air. Meditating before you begin yoga poses will allow you to feel the full benefits of the poses. Like most activities, meditation becomes easier the more you practice it. Meditating for even a short time each day will help your mind and body in many ways.

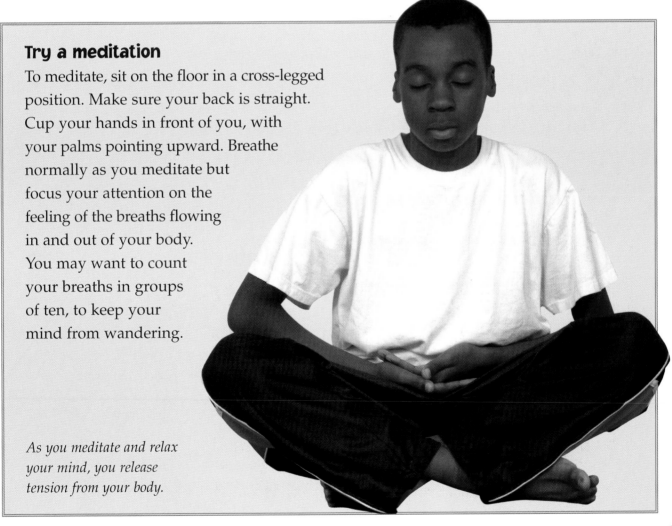

Try a meditation

To meditate, sit on the floor in a cross-legged position. Make sure your back is straight. Cup your hands in front of you, with your palms pointing upward. Breathe normally as you meditate but focus your attention on the feeling of the breaths flowing in and out of your body. You may want to count your breaths in groups of ten, to keep your mind from wandering.

As you meditate and relax your mind, you release tension from your body.

Mountain Pose

*To perform Mountain Pose, stand with your feet together. Move your hips slightly forward to tuck in your **tailbone**. Relax your shoulders and allow your arms to hang by your sides, with your fingers pointing down. Your ears should be directly over your shoulders. Your body should be in a straight line. Hold the pose for ten breaths.*

Many yoga poses, especially poses suitable for young people, imitate things found in nature, such as mountains and trees. They may also imitate the movements of animals. Performing these poses will help you appreciate nature and animals and will keep you healthy and relaxed. The poses shown on pages 12 to 17 are standing poses that will warm up your body. The poses on pages 18 to 27 are sitting poses that will give your body a more challenging and beneficial workout. Your goal should be to perform all the poses in the order that they are shown. You can begin by trying only a few poses and then adding more poses each time you practice.

Standing tall
Mountain Pose is a good pose to learn first because many other poses begin and end in this pose. To do Mountain Pose, stand tall and still. Feel the strength of a mountain inside your body. When you stand in Mountain Pose, your body is **aligned**, or in a perfectly straight line. Standing straight improves your posture. Mountain Pose also helps calm your mind.

Tree Pose

Tree Pose is a standing pose that requires balance and concentration. If you do not concentrate while standing in Tree Pose, you may fall over! Tree Pose increases strength in your legs and flexibility in your hips.

Timber!

When standing in Tree Pose, imagine that your legs and **torso** are a tall, strong tree trunk and that your outstretched arms are leaf-covered branches. If you find it difficult to keep your balance while in Tree Pose, concentrate on your **supporting foot**, or the foot on which you are standing. Imagine that your supporting foot has roots that grow down into the ground to help hold you tall and upright. To help you stay balanced, you can also choose an object in the room on which to focus.

1. Begin Tree Pose by standing in Mountain Pose. Inhale as you raise your right foot. Place the bottom of that foot against the inside of your left thigh. If you find this position too difficult, place your foot anywhere between the ankle and thigh of your left leg.

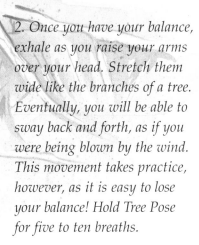

2. Once you have your balance, exhale as you raise your arms over your head. Stretch them wide like the branches of a tree. Eventually, you will be able to sway back and forth, as if you were being blown by the wind. This movement takes practice, however, as it is easy to lose your balance! Hold Tree Pose for five to ten breaths.

13

Warrior II Pose

Warrior II Pose is a standing pose that gives you strength and **determination**. Determination is the ability to follow through with whatever you want to do. In Warrior II Pose, your body position resembles a strong, focused warrior who is ready for battle. Performing Warrior II Pose strengthens and tones the muscles in your legs, hips, back, and arms. It also gives you a warrior's confidence!

Warrior II is a yoga pose that takes time to perfect. To do this pose, imagine that your legs are made of stone. They will feel stiff and strong. If your arms become tired as you perform Warrior II Pose, place your hands on your hips to give your arms a rest. If you find it difficult to keep your balance, practice Warrior II near a wall and touch the wall when you start to lose your balance.

1. To perform Warrior II Pose, begin in Mountain Pose. Take a large step to the side with your left foot. Turn your left foot until your toes are pointing to the left. Turn your right foot slightly in the same direction. Then raise your arms to the side, at shoulder level.

2. Inhale and then exhale as you bend your left knee over your left ankle. Be sure that your knee is not bent beyond your ankle.

3. Turn your head to the left and look out over your left hand. Hold the pose for five breaths and then perform the pose to the right side.

Eagle Pose

Eagle Pose is a challenging balance pose. It requires you to balance on one foot, in the same way that an eagle balances as it perches in a tree or on a rock. Eagle Pose stretches out the muscles in your upper back, as an eagle does when it stretches out its long wings. The pose also stretches your outer thighs and increases your **endurance**. Endurance is the ability to continue an activity, even when it is difficult.

1. Begin in Mountain Pose. Inhale as you raise your arms to shoulder level in front of you. Wrap your right arm underneath your left arm. Exhale as you continue to twist your arms around each other, until your palms are touching. Your hands should be in front of your nose.

2. Inhale, bend your knees slightly, and cross your right thigh over your left thigh. Do not twist your hips as you cross your legs. Your hips should be pointing forward.

3. Exhale as you hook your right foot behind your left calf. Make sure your back is straight. To help keep your balance, choose something in the room on which to focus your attention.

Frog Pose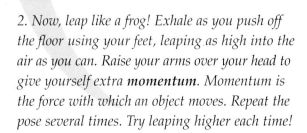

Many yoga poses are **static poses**. Static poses have little motion. They require you to concentrate and allow your body to stretch into the poses slowly. Other poses are **dynamic poses**. Dynamic poses are energetic and use movements to stretch and strengthen your muscles. They also strengthen your heart. Frog Pose combines static and dynamic poses. It moves from a static squat to a dynamic leap. Frog Pose strengthens your legs and ankles, opens your hips, and gives you a great boost of energy!

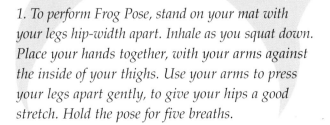

1. To perform Frog Pose, stand on your mat with your legs hip-width apart. Inhale as you squat down. Place your hands together, with your arms against the inside of your thighs. Use your arms to press your legs apart gently, to give your hips a good stretch. Hold the pose for five breaths.

2. Now, leap like a frog! Exhale as you push off the floor using your feet, leaping as high into the air as you can. Raise your arms over your head to give yourself extra **momentum**. *Momentum is the force with which an object moves. Repeat the pose several times. Try leaping higher each time!*

Downward Dog Pose

1. To perform Downward Dog Pose, kneel on **all fours**, or your hands and knees. Your hands should be directly below your shoulders, and your knees should be beneath your hips. Raise your heels and place your toes on the floor.

People can learn a lot about stretching by watching the movements of animals. Copying the ways in which animals stretch feels great! Have you ever seen a dog stretch after waking from a nap? This position is the position in which your body should be while doing Downward Dog Pose. Downward Dog Pose stretches the backs of your legs, while strengthening your arms, shoulders, chest, and back. When in Downward Dog Pose, you can bark like a dog to increase your energy and to exercise the muscles in your throat.

It's all in the legs

Downward Dog Pose can be tricky to perform. You may find that your arms get tired quickly. To help take weight off your arms, shift your hips back so that more of your weight is over your legs. One way to shift your weight is to press your heels against the floor.

2. Inhale and then exhale as you press the palms of your hands into the floor and lift up your hips as far as possible. Straighten your legs, keeping your back straight. Gently press your heels toward the floor. Your head should be relaxed. Breathe deeply for ten breaths and then return to all fours.

Cat Pose

Cats are flexible, graceful animals. Performing Cat Pose will help you improve the flexibility of your spine and will give your shoulders and back a good stretch. Cat Pose also allows you to practice coordinating your breathing with your movements, which is one of the most important lessons you can learn from yoga.

1. To perform Cat Pose, begin on all fours. Your hands should be directly below your shoulders, and your knees should be beneath your hips. Your toes should be pointing back behind you, and your back should be straight.

2. Inhale and then exhale as you press your hands into your mat. Move your hips forward and round your back, pushing your spine up toward the ceiling. Tuck your chin into your chest. Pretend you are a cat stretching after a nap. Hold this position for five breaths.

3. Next, inhale as you arch your back in the opposite direction. Tilt your tailbone up toward the ceiling and raise your head. Your back should be curved toward the floor. Hold this position for five breaths.

Lion Pose

Lions are powerful animals that roar loudly when they are about to attack. Lion Pose is a fun, noisy yoga pose that will energize your entire body! Performing Lion Pose benefits your face, jaw, and throat, which are parts of your body that are not often exercised. Roaring like a lion also releases tension in your chest, and it builds self-confidence. Practice Lion Pose any time you feel that your energy level needs a boost!

1. To perform Lion Pose, sit on your heels with your knees apart. Lean forward as you place your hands on the floor in front of you, with your fingers pointing toward your feet. Inhale as you tilt your head back.

2. Exhale as you stick out your tongue. If you want to, you can try roaring like a lion!

Relaxation Pose

Many people find that Relaxation Pose is their favorite pose to perform. Relaxation Pose allows the **circulation** of the blood in your body to return to normal. For example, when you perform dynamic poses, your heart begins to beat quickly. A fast heartbeat causes your blood to move quickly through your body. Performing Relaxation Pose slows down your heart and allows your blood to move through your body at a normal rate. It is a good idea to perform Relaxation Pose more than once during your practice. You can do it in the middle of your practice to slow down your mind and regain your concentration. Then perform it again at the end of your practice to allow your circulation to return to a normal rate.

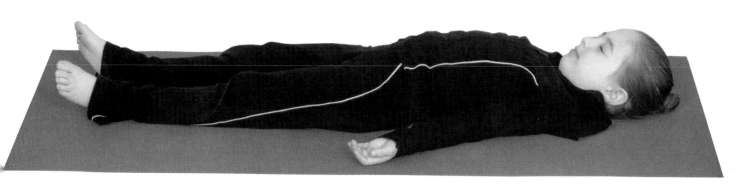

To perform Relaxation Pose, lie on your back with your legs stretched out. Your feet should be about hip-distance apart. Relax your legs so that your feet fall to the side. Your hands should be resting on the floor at your sides, with your palms up. Close your eyes and breathe deeply, allowing your entire body to relax. Your mind should be calm and clear. Remain in this position for as long as you like.

Cobra Pose

Snakes have strong, flexible spines, which allow them to slither up trees or along the ground. When they feel threatened, cobra snakes face their attackers, lift up the front end of their bodies, and hiss. Performing Cobra Pose will help you develop a spine that is strong and flexible like the spine of a cobra snake. It will also help you breathe freely. To make the pose more fun, you can hiss as you raise yourself into Cobra Pose.

1. Lie face-down on your mat. Your legs should be together, so that your body resembles the long, thin body of a snake at rest. Inhale and place your hands underneath your shoulders, with your fingers pointing forward. Keep your elbows close to your body.

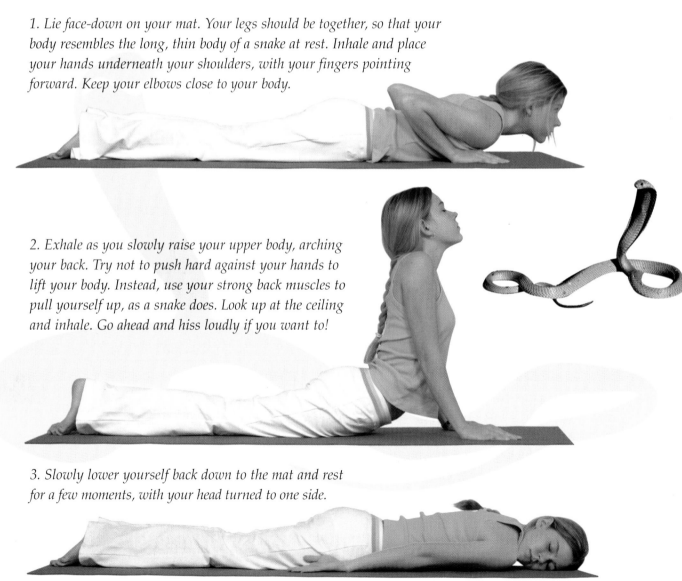

2. Exhale as you slowly raise your upper body, arching your back. Try not to push hard against your hands to lift your body. Instead, use your strong back muscles to pull yourself up, as a snake does. Look up at the ceiling and inhale. Go ahead and hiss loudly if you want to!

3. Slowly lower yourself back down to the mat and rest for a few moments, with your head turned to one side.

Bow Pose

Bow Pose requires you to raise both the upper and lower parts of your body off the floor at the same time. In Bow Pose, your body forms the curved shape of a bow, such as the one shown right. Performing this pose will strengthen your back muscles and help increase the flexibility of your spine. When your spine is flexible, you can bend your body easily in any direction. It is a good idea to follow Cobra Pose and Bow Pose with a **counter pose**, such as Child's Pose (see page 31). A counter pose is a pose that stretches your body in the opposite way. For example, a forward bend is a counter pose to a backbend.

1. Lie face-down on your mat. Inhale as you bend your knees, bringing your feet toward your bottom. Reach your hands back and grab your feet or your ankles.

2. Exhale as you lift your legs up and back. Keep your arms straight. Stretch your upper body back toward your feet. Hold the pose for three to five breaths and then relax.

Tortoise Pose

Tortoises are quiet, slow-moving animals. They carry heavy shells. This may seem like a burden, but the shells provide the tortoises with safe, quiet places in which to sleep and hide from predators. Performing Tortoise Pose will allow you to experience the safe, quiet feeling a tortoise has when it has **retreated**, or drawn itself, into its shell. Tortoise Pose gives your hips and spine a deep, long stretch.

1. Sit on your mat, facing your partner. Bend your knees and spread your feet wider than shoulder-width apart.

2. Inhale and then exhale as you lean forward and slide your arms under your knees. Grab the outside of your feet with your hands. Straighten your legs as much as possible and lower your forehead toward the floor. Stretch only as far as you can without feeling pain.

"Hello, friend!"

It is not easy to stay inside your tortoise shell for long, so many people enjoy doing Tortoise Pose with a partner. Performing the pose with a partner allows you to relax briefly as you peek out of your shell to say "hello" to your partner.

3. Whenever you feel you need a break from the stretch, slowly raise your head and poke it out of your tortoise shell. Smile and say "hello" to your partner!

Cross-Legged Twist Pose

Cross-Legged Twist Pose helps develop flexibility in your spine. Cross-Legged Twist Pose is a counter pose to backbends, such as Cobra Pose or Bow Pose. As you twist in Cross-Legged Twist Pose, make sure both your **sit bones** remain firmly on the floor. Your sit bones are the two bones in your bottom on which you sit. If you lift one of your sit bones off the floor, you will be twisting from your hips. Your goal is to twist from your spine.

1. Sit cross-legged on your mat. Keeping your sit bones on the floor, place your left hand on your right knee.

2. Place your right arm behind you on the floor. Turn your head to the right and look over your right shoulder. Keep your back straight. Hold the pose for five breaths and then repeat on the other side.

Cowface Pose

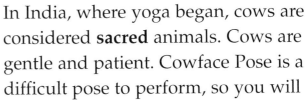

In India, where yoga began, cows are considered **sacred** animals. Cows are gentle and patient. Cowface Pose is a difficult pose to perform, so you will need patience as you learn to perform it. Cowface Pose stretches many parts of your body, including your hips, thighs, shoulders, chest, and even your ankles!

Beginner benefits

When in Cowface Pose, it is important to keep both your sit bones on the floor. If you find the leg position too uncomfortable or difficult, try sitting on a folded towel or blanket.

Can you see the cow's face? Look at yourself in a mirror as you perform Cowface Pose. Imagine what you would look like upside down. Your feet are the cow's horns. Do you see it now?

1. To perform Cowface Pose, sit on your mat with your knees bent and your feet in front of you. Inhale and bend your right leg, pulling it under your left leg until your right foot is next to your left hip.

2. Exhale as you cross your left leg over your right leg, so that your left foot is next to your right hip. Your knees should be one on top of the other. Your bottom knee should be in line with the center of your body.

3. Inhale as you raise your left arm into the air. Your back should be straight. Exhale as you bend your left arm until your hand is at the back of your neck. Then reach your right arm behind you and grab the fingers of your left hand. Hold the pose for five to ten breaths. Then repeat the pose on the other side. You may find that you can touch hands more easily on one side than on the other.

Yoga in motion

A **vinyasa** is a series of dynamic yoga poses that flows from one pose to the next. You can perform a vinyasa at the beginning of your practice to get the energy you need to hold challenging poses. You can also perform a vinyasa at the end of your practice, when your body is warm and flexible from the poses you have already done. Vinyasas are fun and energizing. You can alternate vinyasas with static poses to keep yourself motivated. A great vinyasa to start with is Salute to the Sun, which is shown on these two pages.

1. Begin in Mountain Pose. Bring your palms together in front of your chest. This position is called Prayer Pose.

2. Inhale and stretch your arms over your head. Keep your elbows shoulder-width apart. Lean back slightly.

3. Exhale as you bend forward from the hips. Place your hands on the floor, bending your knees if necessary. Try to keep your back and knees straight.

4. Inhale as you extend your right leg behind you. Lift your chin and look straight ahead.

5. Extend your other leg behind you, so your body is in a straight line. Balance on your toes. If this is too difficult, place your knees on the floor.

6. Exhale as you lower your upper body slowly to the floor.

7. Inhale and move into Cobra Pose.

8. Exhale as you lift your hips and move into Downward Dog Pose.

9. Inhale as you bring your right foot forward. Place it between your hands. Lift your chin and look straight ahead.

10. Exhale as you bring your left foot forward and place it beside your right foot. Your hands should be on the floor in front of you. Keep your back and knees straight, if possible.

11. Inhale and stretch your arms forward as you raise your upper body into a standing position. Raise your arms over your head and lean back slightly.

12. Exhale as you lower your arms down to the side, into Mountain Pose. Bring your hands back into Prayer Pose to finish the vinyasa.

Rest and relaxation

End your yoga practice with some resting poses that help you completely relax your body. Two great resting poses are Relaxation Pose and Child's Pose. Performing these poses at the end of your yoga practice, or at any time during the day, helps your body adjust from being active to being at rest. These poses will also give you time to enjoy the peaceful state of mind created by yoga.

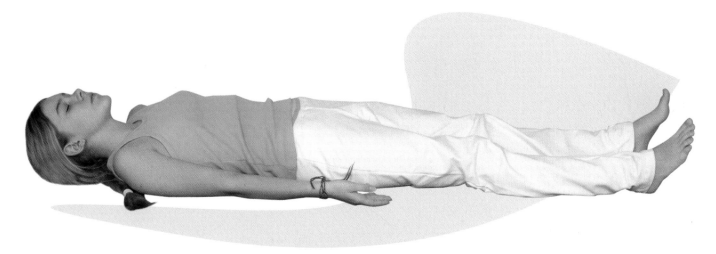

It is important to perform Relaxation Pose at the end of your practice. It helps cool down and relax your body. Turn to page 21 to review the steps in Relaxation Pose.

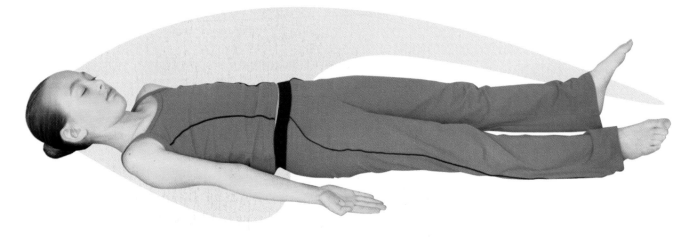

1. Child's Pose gently stretches your hips, thighs, and ankles. It is called Child's Pose because it is a position in which a baby often sleeps. To perform Child's Pose, sit on your mat with your feet tucked under your bottom.

2. Slowly bend forward and place your forehead on the floor. Allow your arms to rest on the floor at your sides with your palms up. If you prefer, you can hold the soles of your feet with your hands. Breathe deeply and allow your body to relax completely. Remain in this position for as long as you feel comfortable.

Glossary

Note: Boldfaced words that are defined in the text may not appear in the glossary.

asanas The physical poses used in Hatha Yoga

abdomen The part of the body between the chest and the hips

certified To be properly trained and qualified to teach

circulation The movement of blood to different parts of the body

devotion A strong feeling of loyalty to a person or group

flexible Able to bend easily into various positions

joint A part of the body where two bones come together; elbows and knees are joints

meditation An exercise in which you focus your mind and allow your thoughts to slow down

oxygen A colorless, odorless gas in the air that people and animals need to breathe

posture The position of a person's body when standing or sitting

principle A basic truth or belief

sacred Describing something that deserves respect

sage A wise and respected person

tailbone The bone at the bottom of the spine

torso The human body, not including the head, the arms, or the legs

Index

1 2 3 4 5 6 7 8 9 0 Printed in the U.S.A. 4 3 2 1 0 9 8 7 6 5